The Passion, Resurrection and Ascension of Jesus Christ According to the Four Gospels

The Passion, Resurrection and Ascension of Jesus Christ According to the Four Gospels

A Poetic Meditation

RAINBOW CHANG

Foreword by
GEORGE PATTISON

RESOURCE *Publications* · Eugene, Oregon

THE PASSION, RESURRECTION AND ASCENSION OF JESUS CHRIST ACCORDING TO THE
FOUR GOSPELS
A Poetic Meditation

Resource Publications
An Imprint of Wipf and Stock Publishers
199 W. 8th Ave., Suite 3
Eugene, OR 97401

www.wipfandstock.com

PAPERBACK ISBN: 978-1-7252-5761-0
HARDCOVER ISBN: 978-1-7252-5762-7
EBOOK ISBN: 978-1-7252-5763-4

Manufactured in the U.S.A.   12/11/19

Foreword

Rainbow Chang's *Passion Resurrection and Ascension of Jesus Christ* stands in a long tradition of Christian meditations on the climactic days of Christ's life on earth, from the Last Supper through, in this case to resurrection and ascension. Its most immediate models are the kinds of liturgical musical settings familiar from the great passions, pre-eminently Bach's, of the Baroque era. Certainly, it is a work that cries out for musical and liturgical performance. Its texts evoke manifold musical resonances, from the spiritual songs of Black American slaves to contemporary hymnody. Indeed, it is a text so suffused with the spirit of Christian music that it is already musical. To read it is to sing it. At the same time, it is a work that is intensely pictorial, presenting a sequence of images, some deeply rooted in tradition, some engagingly new, offering a gallery of visual approaches to the mystery that is its subject.

As the work of a Chinese woman who has embraced Christianity with a profound intensity, it is an exploration that brings new perspectives on an old story, not least the use of the Haiku form and allusions to the aesthetic of cherry-blossom viewing in Japanese culture. At the same time it is attentive to the Jewishness of Yeshua, also drawing on Jewish liturgical prayer. In such ways it is not only a contemporary reworking of a traditional model but also a work for our global society in which, to evoke St Paul, neither East or West alone defines our relation to Christ and both East and West are together essential for creating whatever new paradigm of faith the future will bring—as it surely will. The closing evocation of the great commission prior to the Ascension, that is, the call to 'Go and make disciples of all nations' emphasizes this global movement, encapsulated in the work's final prayer and declaration of commitment: 'Send me, oh send me, I shall go forth to the end of the earth /To proclaim the Word of God on the Cross!'

If what I have said suggests that this is a work that merely plays with cultural forms in an eclectic way, this would be to give a totally wrong impression. This is a work that, from the opening lines, is open to the raw terror and confusion of what confronts us in the passion narrative, it explores the mystery of evil, and the conflict of heaven and hell. Pain, mourning, and grief and given their due – but they are not given the last word.

I have said that *The Passion, Resurrection and Ascension of Jesus Christ* has an essentially liturgical and musical character, but it is subtitled 'a poetic meditation' and it is, in the end, an intensely personal work that will speak as much to the individual reader as to the liturgical assembly, a meditation to foster an further each Christian's ongoing meditation into the meaning and scope of all that happened during those few days, far away and long ago.

George Pattison
University of Glasgow

While I was studying theology in Oxford, I discovered the theological works of the Swiss theologian Han Urs von Balthasar. My PhD proposal for the year of 2015 was to fulfil what Balthasar has said in the forward of his monumental treatise The Glory of the Lord—A Theological Aesthetics, I quote: "The overall scope of the present work naturally remains all too Mediterranean. The inclusion of other cultures, especially that of Asia, it would have been important and fruitful. But the author's education has not allowed for such an expansion, and a superficial presentation of such material would have been dilettantism. May those qualified come to complete the present fragment." I thought I was the one who is qualified to engage with what Balthasar has done and argue for an integrated theological aesthetics of the Glory of the Lord with my knowledge in Oriental theatre, arts, literature, philosophy and religion. I could have completed my thesis by now, but I did not even start this PhD project as I became pregnant a few months before the start of the course and became a single mother when my daughter was only three months old. I decided to take full responsibility for my child, and that was the end of my PhD project.

I lost my privilege to sit in the beautiful libraries of Oxford as a fulltime mother. My daily life was filled with taking her to early education groups, play groups, playground, grocery shopping, cooking, washing, cleaning, nappy changing and of course I breast fed her until she was 2 years and 10 months old. I used to get up 4 times or more every night until she was 2 years and three months old. Every time pass by the Old Bodleian library with my daughter where I used to sit, read and write, my tears always fill my eyes. Yes, we could not do research without a good library but our minds, hearts and souls are always free to meditate on the beauty, truth and Goodness of God's Incarnated Word even when we are walking our children in the pram. Yes, we could not write a theological treatise without references and quotations but we can write poetry in our head and on our smart phones while shopping in a grocery store or sitting in a children's playgroup with our children. The love of God just could not stop overflowing from our hearts because our hearts are only a small container inside of a big container for the love of God, and this big container is the hearts of all God's Children, it will overflow one way or another from us to others as we are born to share this love. This small work I have written is a way of the love of God in me overflowing in result of my life circumstances. It was done with great practical difficulties, but the Grace of God was above it. Just to give you one example, one morning, I was on my knee to ask God give me the real understanding of the Cross so that I could put it into poetic words, I was so desperate to understand, so I said: 'I shall not get up unless you let me understand.' Then, less than ten minute later, I had to get up as my child was in need of me. I have surely fallen short of the Glory of the Lord in my life and in this work but I trust that God's Grace covers it all.

This poetic meditation is written as a liturgical music drama which I shall set music and stage it after its publication. It consists two forms of poetry: Japanese Haiku and Western lyric poetry. There are theology and aesthetic ideas reflected in this small work, which I may explore further in a systematic form in the near future, but for now, it is not the time for me to explain, it is the time for you to read.

A special thanks to Arabella Elizabeth Stell, who is my beloved three years old daughter. Thank you for praying with me together every day and night. You have been saying "Amen" at the end of each prayer since you were one year old. After I sing the Jesus Prayer, you would say, mummy, now it's my turn, and sing better than mummy. Thank you for accompanying me to the Holy Land and Japan during my writing. Your little feet walked around with me in the Old City of Jerusalem even though I carried you most of the time, and I got to see where Jesus's body was laid in the tomb inside of the Holy Sepulchre without waiting in the long queue because of you, who were only two years old. You even came out of the pram for one minute and helped me to push the pram when I was pushing you in the pram on Mount Olive with such difficulty. You endured most of the long silence of a Japanese tea ceremony in Kyoto; you only broke the silence and said "more, more, more" after the tea biscuits were all eaten by you. You graciously only picked up a few of the gravels which raked to represent the ripples of water in the Gardens in Kyoto and threw them into the lake, otherwise, I would probably still be imprisoned on your behalf in Japan. Thank you for being so good with your sweet and long sleeps as I wrote some of these poems while you were doing that. This poetic meditation would have not existed without the existence of you. I pray that one day you will also sing your own new song to the Lord in whatever form you may choose, and realise why your mummy often wept and wept when she reads the Bible stories to you in the early years of your life---it was for the Beauty of the Lord revealed in the words of the Holy Scriptures, she wept and wept.

Rainbow Chang, May 2019, Oxford

The Passion, Resurrection and Ascension of Jesus Christ

According to the Four Gospels

------A Poetic Meditation

Rainbow Chang

Prelude

In the Beginning

Were you there when God said there shall be light
Were you there when God formed the sky, moon, stars, created the
earth, mountains and the sea
Were you there to see the first sun rise shining over lion and lamb
running side by side
Were you there when the first flower opening its bud on earth and the
lark ascending into sky
Were you there in the dance of water from ocean to clouds and back
Were you the music the first man and woman sang when they came into
life
Were you the blanket of love covering us before we opened our eyes
Were you the longing that we were all born for
The longing to be alive
Were you the word that spoke first
So that we can shout for joy
Cry for hope
Were you there when God said there shall be light
And there was light

1. The Lord's Supper

Opening Prayer
----------Sh'ma Yisrael[1]

Hear, Israel, the Lord is our God, the Lord is one
Blessed be the Name of His glorious kingdom for ever and ever
And you shall love the Lord your God with all your heart and with all your
soul and with all your might

Hear, Israel, the Lord is our God, the Lord is one
Blessed be the Name of His glorious kingdom for ever and ever
And you shall love the Lord your God with all your heart and with all your
soul and with all your might

---

[1] Deuteronomy 6:4-5

The night God protected it[2]
The House of Israel redemption from slavery
The power of God alive

---

[2] I wrote these lines in Japanese Haiku form

They sat under cherry-blossom tree[3]
Sounds of water, birds, and psalm praises
Seder plate flavours of life

---

[3] I wrote these lines in Japanese Haiku form

The Song of Archangel Michael who is the protector of Israel and the Christian Church

Remember not only the departing of the red sea, oh Israel
Remember the grace of deliverance
Remember not only the ram in place of Issac, oh Israel
Remember the mercy of redemption
Remember not only the time of the past, oh Israel
Remember the time is here, now and near
Open your eyes and see, Oh Israel
Open your eyes and look into the future, Oh Israel

First Eucharist Song: Calling to the Table of Christ

There should be enough bread for every soul to eat on earth
But you have eaten your brother's bread
So that I came down from heaven to feed the hungry
Come to my table, oh the past
Come to my table, oh the now
Come to my table, oh the future
Come to my table, oh the south
Come to my table, oh the north
Come to my table, oh the west
Come to my table, oh the east
Come to my table, you, my dear friend
Take and eat
This is my body
The bread of life
Eat and you shall be hungry no more
Take and eat,
This is my body
The manna of heaven
Eat and you shall have eternal life
Take and eat
This is my flesh
The flesh of the Passover Lamb takes away the sins of the world and
gives new life
Eat and you shall be part of me which surpasses imagination and reason

There should be no thirst in this world
But you have not only drunk your brother's water
You have drunk your brother's life
So that I came down from above and poured out my blood
To wash away the sins of the world, to cease all thirst
You who stabbed lives to death in London
You who sold poisoned baby milk powder in China
You who traded blood diamond

You who trafficked women and children
You who took war on other countries for your own gains
Repent and Come to my table
Take and drink
Drink this cup of my blood
The blood of power and love
It cleanses you within, all the sins to pass
With a pure heart you shall be joining the choir of angels to sing
hallelujah
Come, you, come
Repent and come to my table
Drink this cup of my blood
The blood of power and love
It cleanses you within, all the sins to pass
You shall be joyfully in me the living water
Come, you, come
Repent and come to my table
Drink this cup of my blood
The blood of power and love
It cleanses you within, all the sins to pass
You will be longing to love as I have loved you

Come to my table as often as you can
Take and eat my body
Take and drink my blood
So that you can be part of me
So that you can remember who I am, what I have done and what I shall
do
So that you can recognize where I am now
So that you can become part of me
Come to my table as often as you can
All of you and no one shall be turned away
Come to this heavenly feast on earth which transcend time and space
Come to this table of love
In remembrance of me, Jesus of Nazareth, the King of the Jews

Psalm 13:

Praise the Lord
Praise, O servants of the Lord
Praise the name of the Lord
Let the name of the Lord be praised
Both now and forever more
From the rising of the sun to the place where it sets
The name of the Lord is to be praised
The Lord is exalted over all the nations

Abram our father, Joseph's bone[4]
Twelve tribes of Israel now the twelve
Betrayal both ancient and new

The night to be guarded [5]
The lamb of God redemption of man
The permitted betrayal of Jesus

---

[5] I wrote these lines in Japanese Haiku form

The Song of Samael who is the archangel of death, the accuser of Israel

Why should dust turn into man
It is not right
Why should grace overcome nature
It is not lawful
Why should mercy overcome sin
It is not just
I am the king of death therefore I do not need to know life
Even the goodness and faithfulness of Job can become the reasons of
my accusation
With the logic of the self I tempted Adam and Eve
I have no need to see the light as I am blind
With blind eyes you have received the dipped bread at the table of Jesus
the Nazarene

2. Gethsemane

The night to be guarded[6]
A lonely teacher with twelve sleeping disciples
Heavy eyes this Gethsemane night

---

[6] I wrote these lines in Japanese Haiku form

Jesus overwhelmed with sorrow[7]
In Gethsemane drops of blood he prays
This cup will of the Father

---

[7] I wrote these lines in Japanese Haiku form

Mount of Olives Jesus arrested[8]
Smell of fresh leaves kiss of Juda
Sound of fear disciples scattered

---

[8] I wrote these lines in Japanese Haiku form

Th Song of an Angel Strengthening Jesus in Gethsemane

Be strong and courageous
For you choose to drink this cup of wrath for the redemption of your
people
Be strong and courageous
For you desire to go into the land of death and carry your people to the
land of life on the wings of love
Be strong and courageous
For your compassion for the suffering of your people is as strong as
death so that you shall die on the Cross
Be strong and courageous
For you know the hour has really come
Be strong and courageous Yeshua God's begotten Son

The Song of Yeshua

It is the time to say goodbye
To the ones I have loved in my mortal flesh
I will remember my mother's breast
Her milk I drank as a baby
Her milk with warmth and love

It is the time to say goodbye
To the ones I have loved in my mortal flesh
I still remember the children of Israel running around on the street of
Jerusalem
The friendship I have made with young and old

It is the time to say goodbye
To the ones I have loved in my mortal flesh
I still remember the setting sun and rising moon on the sea of Galilee
The taste of fish around fire with you

It is the time to say goodbye
To the ones I have loved in my mortal flesh
But the melody of memory never to say goodbye
All the breath of the living has its last
All the green leaves will go dry and fall from the tree
But all and all shall come back to life
As if it wakes up from a dream
As if the spring returns
Every life that breathed its first
Already an everlasting song
The melody of memory
Never to say goodbye
Now, here comes my rest

Judas took thirty silver coins[9]
A price set on Yeshua by Israel
Innocent blood shed blood shed

---

[9] I wrote these lines in Japanese Haiku form

Juda returned the silver coins[10]
He was seized with remorse and repented
He hanged himself he hanged himself

---

[10] I wrote these lines in Japanese Haiku form

27

The Song of Judas

Like a dog
Lost home
Judas, Judas, Judas
Dragging along
His own shadow
Foot steps
Sound of sorrow
Wander around
Under the light of the moon
Smell of blood
Money thrown away
The Son of God has just been laid down
On the cursed ground of Adam
Terror eating up the left-over of a soul
The soul of Judas
In this sleepless night of spring
Dark, dark, dark
What have I done
What have I done
Swallow my tongue
Exchange for an angel's song
Oh, Angels of above
Falling down to earth
I want to sing a new song

Avinu Malkeinu[11]

Our Father, Our King, we have sinned before you
Our Father, our King, we have no King but you
Our Father, our king, act with us for the sake of Your Name
Our Father, our king, withhold the plague from your inheritance
Our Father, our King, pardon and forgive all our iniquities
Our Father, our King, blot out and remove our transgressions from
before your eyes
Our Father, our King, erase in your abounding mercies all the record of
our sins
Our Father, our King, bring us back to you in wholehearted repentance
Our Father, our King, send a complete healing to the sick of your people
Our Father, our king, rend the evil of the verdict decreed against us
Our Father, our King, remember us with a favorable remembrance
before you

---

[11] Hebrew Prayer Book

Kadish Prayer[12]

May His great name be exalted and sanctified
In the world which He created according to His will.
May He establish His kingdom and may His salvation blossom and His
anointed be near during your lifetime of all the House of Israel
Speedily and very soon! And say Amen!
May the prayers and supplications of all Israel be accepted by their
father who is in heaven and say Amen!
May there be abundant peace from heaven and good life, satisfication,
help, comfort, refuge, healing, redemption, forgiveness, atonement, relief
and salvation for us and for all his people Israel, and say Amen!
May he who makes peace in His high places grant in His mercy upon us
and upon all Israel and say Amen!

---

[12] Hebrew Prayer Book

3. Before Pilate

Kyoto cherry blossom spring air[13]
Yeshua was led to Pilate in Jerusalem
Birds singing high and low

[13] I wrote these lines in Japanese Haiku form

The Zen master of Kyoto[14]
Is making neat sea waves with gravel
He asked what is truth

---

[14] I wrote these lines in Japanese Haiku form

Pilate Yeshua face to face[15]
Shouting, tension, politics, power, the human drama
He asked what is truth

What is truth

The tear of suffering is true
But suffering is not the truth
The sorrow of death is true
But death is not the truth
Injustice temporarily dominating the earth is true
But injustice is not the truth
There are many philosophical ideas about the truth is true
But philosophical ideas are not the truth
Mother giving birth to life is true
But mother is not the truth
The sun rising and setting every day is true
But the sun is not the truth
Then
What is the truth
Pilate asked Yeshua

Yeshua replied
I am the truth
I am the truth
I am the truth

How absurd
I thought truth is beyond my reach

Yes, that is true
And that's the reason why the truth came down to earth
Walked among us
Ate, breathed and faced death like one of us

Pilate was face to face with the truth but did not recognise him
The question remains
What is truth
Truth exist is true
But truth is not truth until you see truth exist and recognise that He is the
truth

4. Crucifixtion

Beauty was mocked by ugly[16]
Humiliated King was torched by his people
To Journey and be slayed

---

[16] I wrote these lines in Japanese Haiku form

On the Mount of Skull[17]
His body was hanging on the tree
Blossom mixed with blood smell

[17] I wrote these lines in Japanese Haiku form

The Sweetest Goodbye

I remember the Sh'ma you used to sing to me
When I was so tiny and small
Oh mother
The twinkling stars of night
The moon light shone through your eyes
How sweet was the melody of Sh'ma and the taste of your breast milk
How warm was to sleep in your loving arms
With angels of music playing harps around us
I remember the Sh'ma you used to sing to me
When I was so tiny and small
Oh, my dear mother
Close your eyes and do not cry
See this tree I am nailed on from your inner eyes
See it as it is a tree full of cherry blossom
And a bird's nest is penetrating the songs of new life
Close your eyes and do not cry
My dear mother
Sing once more the Sh'ma to me just like I was about to sleep when I
was a baby boy
That will be the sweetest goodbye
Sing once more Sh'ma my dear mother
That will be the sweetest goodbye to your dear son

Sh'ma Yisrael[18]

(Hebrew: Sh'ma Yisrael Adonai Eloheinu Adonai Echad
Barukh sheim k'vod malkhuto l'olam va'ed
V'ahav'ta eit Adonai Elohekha b'khol l'vav'kha uv'khol naf'sh'kha uv'khol
m'odekha
Sh'ma Yisrael Adonai Eloheinu Adonai Echad
Sh'ma Yisrael Adonai Eloheinu Adonai Echad)

Hear, Israel, the Lord is our God, the Lord is one
Blessed be the Name of His glorious kingdom for ever and ever
And you shall love the Lord your God with all your heart and with all your
soul and with all your might

Hear, Israel, the Lord is our God, the Lord is one
Blessed be the Name of His glorious kingdom for ever and ever
And you shall love the Lord your God with all your heart and with all your
soul and with all your might

---

[18] Hebrew Prayer Book

The Song of Angels Around The Cross of Christ

One drop, two drops, three drops, 10 drops
Of precious blood of God made flesh
One drop, two drops, three drops, 10 drops
Of precious blood of pure love
One drop, two drops, three drops, 10 drops
Of precious blood of mercy
One drop, two drops, three drops, 10 drops
Of precious blood of power over Sin and death
One drop, two drops, three drops, 10 drops
Of precious blood of the Messiah poured out
For you on the Cross
Drink this final cup of Passover wine
For your redemption is here

Yeshua breathed his last breath[19]
He said that it is finished finished
Blood, tears on his face

---

[19] I wrote these lines in Japanese Haiku form

10 Strings Harp

Made with Adam's apple tree and the bone of Yeshua
Made from when time began to this very moment
Waited, thousands of years, oh here you are, Israel
Hanging on the mount of Skull, it is the 10 strings harp
Remember, Adam's sorrow
Remember, Issac's hopelessness
Remember, why this night is different from other nights
Sh'ma Yisrael
Gently, the wind of creation blew
On this bleeding body and soul and divinity—the10 strings harp
Quietly, music rising in the four corners of the earth
The melody of beginning in the end
The harmony of life in death
Sh'ma Yisrael
Hear the music of your messiah
In the wind of your ears
Sh'ma Yisrael
Rise up and sing with the choir of angels
For the music of heaven is now dwelling on earth
Shekhinah, shekhinah, shekhinah, shekhinah

Beautifully to Die

Flying back against the time of mind
Flying across the memory of earth
The wings weeping, the wings weeping
Weeping over the apple hanging in the air
Above the city
City of God, city of man
The children of Adam meet in the air
Flipping the wings of birds with the faces of man
Apple could not speak
The above could not hear
Silently passing by, silently passing by
The flipping wings passing to die
To the tree once Adam and Eve ate the apple
To where the story is thought to have begun
To the beginning of the wondering mind
Heaven opened angels falling down
On this cursed ground of Adam
Flipping wings with faces of man to the tree stand
Cry, cry, cry, towards where the apple was hanging
Cry to reach the end of triangle sky the end of hunting eye
Beautifully to die
Beautifully to die

Only in Love Thorn Appears

Depart, depart
The waters of red sea, oh depart
My love, come in
Come in to this deep deep shadow of my splitting soul
Ponder, ponder upon the beauty of this missing dry ground
With nothing to see
Nothing to walk on
Not even a brain
Only only only pain, only pain flipping this blind wing
Only pain flipping this blind wing
With, with thorns of flesh I love you
Open the mouth of skull I call upon your name
Only only in death life remains
Only, only in love thorn appears
Only in death life remains
Only in love thorn appears
Depart, depart, depart the waters of red sea, oh depart
My love, my love, come in

Second Eucharist Song: Entering Into The Life of Christ

Unite with me within oh the Beautiful
Unite with me within oh the Good
Unite with me within oh the Truth
Unite with me within oh as the way it was in the beginning
The beginning of creation

Unite with me within oh this perfect sacrifice
Unite with me within oh this bread of presence
Unite with me within oh this manna of heaven
Unite with me within oh this bread of face
Unite with me within oh this wine pure blood of the divine
Let this new blood of life run through my veins like the joyful water
running in the garden of Eden

Unite with me within oh the suffering Passover Lamb of Israel
Let the memory of the Cross like the brightest sun burning my eyes
Unite with me within oh the Harrowing of Hell
Let this deepest compassion descending into the darkest corner of my
soul
Unite with me within oh the resurrected Son of Man
Let the victory gently rise like the moon of Jerusalem shining over my
mortal flesh
Unite with me within oh the paschal mystery of mysteries
Let the thunder and lightning of heaven break into the barren land of my
blind mind

Unite with me within oh unite with me within
Let me grow into Beauty
Unite with me within oh unite with me within
Let me grow into Good
Unite with me within oh unite with me within
Let me grow into Truth

Unite with me within oh this aching love
Let me grow into fearlessness in time
Unite with me within oh this calling to life, the life eternal
Let my life begin in my answering to your gentle voice within me here and now

Third Eucharist Song: The Choir of Angels---Kedushah[20]

(Hebrew: Kadosh Kadosh Kadosh Adonai Tz'vaot M'lo Khol Ha'aretz K'vodo
Baruch K'vod Adonai Mim'komo
Yimloch Adonai L'Olam, Elohayich Tziyon L'dor Vador Hall'luyah)

Holy, Holy, Holy, The Lord of Hosts, the entire world is filled with His glory
Blessed is the Glory of the Lord in Its place
The Lord shall reign forever, Your God, O Zion, from generation to generation, Hallelujah

[20] Hebrew Prayer Book

The Last Tear of Christ

Dive deep into the tears of Christ on the Cross
The tears of all tears
I want to see the face of ancient days
One question to ask but for millions of pain
Why, why, why, is this horror even allowed to begin
These thousands of years on earth under the shadow of pain pain pain
All tears shall be wiped away in heaven but what about our days on earth
It begins with our mother's painful birth
Even the mother of Incarnated God is not spared
Christ the innocent suffered for us all on the cross
And we suffer with him more afterwards
How could this possibly even make sense

I sit in the last tear on Yeshua's face
Who is hanging on the cross and has just breathed his last breath
Watch darkness cover the whole of earth
Curtain of the temple of God torn part
The earth shakes to pieces
Saints walked out of their graves
Oh, ancient days
I want to see you face to face
The lamb of God takes away the sins of the world
And the world sins against the lamb two thousand years more
How how how to hold on to this precious faith of
Kingdom of God will be on earth as it is in heaven as your Son have taught us

I sit in the last tear on Yeshua's face
Who is hanging on the cross and has just breathed his last breath
If the beauty of ancient days is not to be fully known now
If the mystery of the Cross is not to be fully understood now
Then I shall sit here inside of the last tear of Christ
Until it is fully known

Until it is fully understood
I am weeping inside of the last tear of Christ

5. The Death of Jesus in the Tomb

Dead, wrapped in line cloth[21]
His body lay in a new tomb
King of Jews Joseph's son

Guarded, sealed, the stone tomb[22]
The women outside wept under the moon
Birds sang, the night sky

---

[22] I wrote these lines in Japanese Haiku form

The Death of Jesus In the Tomb

Like a mother
Rather to take on the pain and death of her sick, dying child
God was born into human flesh just like one of us
Like us, He suffered
And was born to face death like all of us
We die with blind eyes in the night
He dies with moonlight in His eyes
This light in Him takes Him to find us in utter darkness--the Hell of all
flesh
When He found us in His death, He was dead like all of us
So that He could take our death on the wings of love flying beyond death
This story is no other than beauty Himself
This act is for no other than the Good Himself
This reason reveals no other than the Truth Himself

The Lamentation of Marry Over Her Son Yeshua

Baruch Hashem, Baruch Hashem
My son Yeshua, my son Yeshua
From heaven you came and to heaven you are gone
But forever you are my son Yeshua
I remember the hour when you were born
I remember the hour when you were dead
The joy and the sorrow are covering the earth
I pour out my soul to Hashem
Its filled with the memory of love and loss
The God of Abraham, Issac and Jacob
Behold my dear son
Baruch Hashem, Baruch Hasem
I can see him no more with these finite eyes
I can touch him no more with these mortal hands
But he forever is my son
My boy who was in my womb and born into human flesh
The tender body of my son
How much I want to hold you once more
Once more cuddle your warm flesh
You might be the God Incarnate
Saviour of the world
The Passover Lamb
The Messiah
The internal atonement of the Sin of Man
Forever you are my son
My son Yeshua my son Yeshua
Baruch Hashem, Baruch Hashem

A Duet Song of Archangel Michael and Satan about the Death of Jesus

Satan: I hear amazing music of silence from Hell

Michael: Hear this amazing music of silence in Hell, Lord Jesus is descending

Satan: I tried to copy this music with the instrument built in my bone, but my attempt has failed, as this music is full of silence, full of love, full of Grace which I could not bear

Michael: This music is full of silence, full of love, the music of Divine Grace which the world could not bear

Satan: I have seen and fought with Michael over the dead body of Moses on mount Nebo, but the dead body of Jesus, I cannot see. I am the prince of this world, there should be nothing beyond my eyes in this world, but I cannot see the dead body of Jesus

Michael: How could the prince of this world see Jesus in His mysterious death, which is truly divine and truly human, truly life and truly death. Be quiet, oh all minds and hearts, listen, listen, listen to Jesus descending into Hell, listen, listen, listen to this amazing music of silence together with the stars of heaven and the flowers of earth and be still, be absolutely still, do not move

6. Resurrection

Empty tomb with angel's wing[23]
Jesus resurrected from death with wounds fresh
Tell others He is alive

The Song of Archangel Michael and Gabriel at the Resurrection

Fear not, for the Jesus you are seeking who was Crucified, dead and buried now has risen to life
Sing a new song with joy and walk no more but dance, oh ye whom He love
Tell His disciples and the whole world that He is alive
Seek no more the living among the dead
Sing a new song with joy and walk no more but dance, oh ye whom He love
For He is alive

The Empty Tomb

Man may have tried millions of times to open the curtain of death to life
But only the Grace of God can lift it up
Like the Sun brings new dawn
The Good news is not what we have done
The Good news is what God has done for us
Rejoice, rejoice
The Resurrection of Christ opens the new day of life on earth
You and me now can walk into the light of Grace
If we are not in the Grace yet
May God put us there
If we are in the Grace already
May God keep us there
Rejoice, rejoice
With our beliefs and doubts
Let's run to see the empty tomb of Jesus

The Song of Doubting Thomas

Do I own this awaking love
It simply appeared for you
It appeared without knowing
I am in the same wonder as you
In the same wonder
The same fear
Have I seen you somewhere somewhere
The silence is overwhelming
I failed to hear where the music all began
The music moves
Moves still
Out of my hands to reach you
Your wound of the Cross
This touch bears too much of fear
Fear of losing you again
Where you have come
Where you are to go
For the failures of memory
I beg you to remember me
When all else fade
Remember me
Lord Jesus

Raise Us Up in Your Resurrection

Lord Jesus, loose our shackled heads in Plato's Cave with compassion
Lord Jesus, lead us out of unexamined life with light
Lord Jesus, bring out our true nature with the truth
Lord Jesus, ease the pain of our eyes in facing the burning sun for the first time with love
Lord Jesus, strengthen our conviction of this new world in front of eyes with power
Lord Jesus, help us to endure the rejection of my brothers in our return to the cave with your wisdom
Lord Jesus raise us up in Your Resurrection
Lord Jesus lift us high in Your Ascension
Lord Jesus Christ, the Son of God, have mercy on us

7. The Ascension

Blessing, rising, singing, in Bethany[24]
Shocking, mazing, wondering, looking, in Jesus's Ascension
Praying, longing, hoping, in faith

---

[24] I wrote these lines in Japanese Haiku form

Ascension Song 1

Standing tall on Mount Oliver
Facing the bright sun light at noon
We barely can see Jerusalem but we know Jerusalem is there
Catching the wind in our hands
Nothing stays but we breathe the fresh air
You said that it is to our advantage that you go away
If that is so, Lord, please go
We know that there are colours hidden in the light of sun
We know that
There is music remaining silent in our ears
We know that
There are places we are not aware of but there
If that is so Lord, please go
Go to the place we cannot go now
And carry us in your heart
We hold onto you not by our hands but in our hearts
Knowing you are there
Knowing you are here
Knowing you are everywhere

Ascension Song 2

Singing with joy earthly choir:
Lift up your heads, oh gates
And be lifted up, oh ancient doors
let the King of Glory come in

Singing with joy heavenly choir:
Lift up your heads, oh, gates,
And be lifted up, oh ancient doors
Let the King of Glory come in

Ascension Song 3

The angels of Lord saying
He shall return just as the way He was gone

The Sun, the Moon, the stars of sky
Await
The mountain, the ocean, the forest of earth
Await
The eagles, the larks, the nightingales of air
await
The earthworms, ants and beetles of soil
Await

The angels of Lords saying
He shall return just as the way He was gone

The nations of the world
Await
The colours of all races
Await
The children of Adam and Eve
Await

The Angels of the Lord saying
He shall return just as the way He was gone
All Creation awaits

Ascension Song 4

Look up at the heavens on the Mount of Olives
You appear just as the way you were
Look up at the heavens from four corners of earth
You appear just as the way you are
Look up at the heavens in ascension with you
You appear just as the way you always will be
Good in Goodness
True in Truth
Beautiful in Beauty
Infinite in finite, finite in infinite
Form in formless, formless in form
The beginning in the end, the end in the beginning
To free and to love
The dance of Life appears and disappears
In perfect harmony
In mysterious rhythm

8. The Great Commission

A mountain green and windy[25]
Jesus met and commissioned all his disciples
The sound of Galilee sea

[25] I wrote these lines in Japanese Haiku form

Song of Mission

Our planet earth is small in the vast galaxy
Among the stars, moon and sun
Our life is short in the millions of time
Among the lives before and after us
From dust we all have come from and to dust we all shall return
Only in You, we find our life in death
There are many things we can do
And there are many things have been done
Adam tailed the earth
Eve gave birth
Only in You we can do our best
Only in You the best we can do
In between the hours of tears
The tears of new life and the tears of death
I shall hold Your Word dear in the depth of my death and life
Let me breathe, speak, move and bless in your story of love
Every breath I breathe out into the air
Every word I let fly from my mouth
Every act I do, I do it with Your courage and love
Every thought I ponder, wonder and remember
It is the Word of God on the Cross
The Word was written with blood and tears in the heaven of a child on earth:
Hear what he says:
"Go and make disciples of all nations
Baptising them in the name of the Father and the Son and the Holy Spirit
And teaching them to obey everything I have commanded you
And surely I am with you always
To the very end of the age."
Many have gone and many will go
Gazing at heaven from a half-closed window on earth
I sing this new song
A song of praise:

Send me oh send me, I shall go forth to the end of the earth
To proclaim the Word of God on the Cross

www.ingramcontent.com/pod-product-compliance
Lightning Source LLC
LaVergne TN
LVHW081326060426
835511LV00011B/1873